EDGE
BOOKS™

BUSTING BOREDOM
WITH EXPERIMENTS

BY JENNIFER SWANSON

CAPSTONE PRESS
– a capstone imprint

Edge Books are published by Capstone Press,
1710 Roe Crest Drive, North Mankato, Minnesota 56003
www.mycapstone.com

Library of Congress Cataloging-in-Publication Data
Names: Swanson, Jennifer, author.
Title: Busting boredom with experiments / by Jennifer Swanson.
Description: North Mankato, Minnesota : Capstone Press, [2017] | Series: Edge
    books. Boredom busters | Audience: Ages 8–14. | Audience: Grades 4 to 6. |
    Includes bibliographical references and index.
Identifiers: LCCN 2016031185 | ISBN 9781515747024 (library binding) | ISBN
    9781515747147 (eBook PDF)
Subjects: LCSH: Science—Experiments—Juvenile literature.
Classification: LCC Q175.2 .S935 2017 | DDC 507.8—dc23
LC record available at https://lccn.loc.gov/2016031185

Acknowledgements
Alesha Sullivan, editor; Kyle Grenz, designer; Morgan Walters, media researcher;
Katy LaVigne, production specialist; Marcy Morin and Sarah Schuette, project
producers

Photo Credits
Capstone Studio: Karon Dubke, 5, 7, 8, 11, 13, 15, 17, 19, 21, 23, 25, 27, 28;
Shutterstock: bioraven, (fruits) Cover, bluebright, (jar) Cover, Bruno Ismael Silva
Alves, (grunge texture) design element throughout, Bryan Solomon, (bottle) Cover,
Clip Art, (eggs) Cover, Hein Nouwens, (timer) Cover, Mickicev Atelje, (measuring
cups) Cover, PictureStudio, (tape measure) Cover, vladis.studio, (glue, scissors, pen)
Cover

Printed and bound in the USA
010027S17

TABLE of CONTENTS

TIME TO DISCOVER

It's a rainy day. School is out for the week. Your sports team is done for the season. You're fresh out of ideas on something to do for fun. Look no further! Have you ever heard of Thomas Edison, Marie Curie, or Albert Einstein? They were once kids just like you. They were also famous scientists who loved to make discoveries. Thomas Edison perfected the lightbulb. Marie Curie experimented with *radioactivity*. Albert Einstein was an influential *physicist*. Perhaps these scientists thought up their ideas when they were bored.

Now it's your turn. Maybe you'll accidentally invent something in the process. Gather some supplies and household items—you're about to bust some boredom with experiments. After all, you could be the next great scientist!

radioactivity—a process in which atoms break apart and create a lot of energy

physicist—a person who studies matter and energy

SAFETY FIRST

Some of these experiments will require adult supervision, while others you'll be able to tackle on your own. Before you begin any project, make sure you have all the required tools and materials, and carefully read all the way through the instructions.

THE SCIENTIFIC METHOD

The scientific method is a set of steps that scientists use to guide them when doing an experiment. It is an organized way to answer questions about how things work in the universe. It contains these basic ideas:

1. Question: Make an observation or ask a question
2. *Hypothesize*: Create an educated guess about why you think something is happening
3. Experiment: Conduct an experiment to test your hypothesis
4. Results: Collect and record the *data* from the experiment
5. Conclusion: Analyze your results to see if your hypothesis was correct or incorrect

hypothesis—a prediction that can be tested about how a scientific investigation or experiment will turn out

data—information or facts

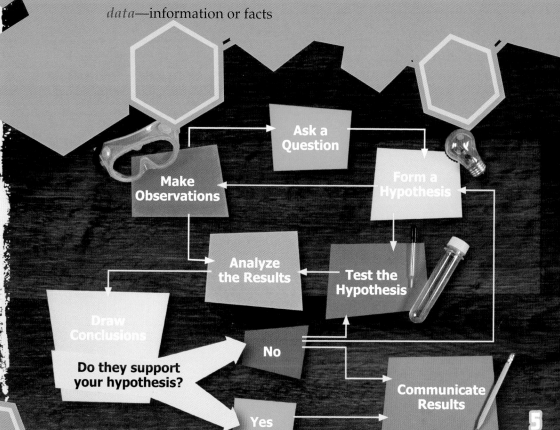

Ask a Question

Make Observations

Form a Hypothesis

Analyze the Results

Test the Hypothesis

Draw Conclusions

Do they support your hypothesis?

No

Yes

Communicate Results

CRA-ACK!

LIGHTNING IN A BOTTLE

MATERIALS

scissors
2 Styrofoam plates
aluminum pie pan
masking tape
glass jar
timer or stopwatch
wool sock or cloth
pen and paper

Have you ever wondered how a lightning bolt occurs? The *energy* that forms when a cold air system and a warm air system meet creates negative charges called electrons. The electrons are attracted to positive charges, called protons, on the ground. The result is a giant spark. Try making your very own lightning bolt! Don't worry—it's only *static electricity*.

1 Cut a 4-inch (10-centimeter) strip of Styrofoam out of one plate.

2 Attach the strip of Styrofoam to the back of the pie pan with masking tape. This is your handle to move the pie pan.

3 Place the glass jar on a table, with the opening facing up.

4 Rub the other Styrofoam plate across the top of your head for two minutes.

energy—the ability to do work, such as moving things or giving heat or light

static electricity—the buildup of an electrical charge on the surface of an object

5 Put the Styrofoam plate on the table.

6 Using the handle, pick up the pie pan and set it on top of the Styrofoam plate. Let it sit for 15 seconds.

7 Using the handle again, pick up the pie pan and place it on top of the jar.

8 Take one finger and touch the outside of the jar. You should see a tiny lightning bolt. Did you feel a tiny jolt?

9 Try this experiment again. This time rub the styrofoam plate across a wool sock instead of your hair.

10 Hypothesize and try different materials to see how many lightning bolts you can create.

11 Record your results in a table, similar to the one below.

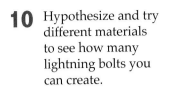

Material used:	Was there a lightning bolt?	How strong was the bolt?
Hair		
Wool sock		

KABOOM!
GAS LEAK IN A BAG

MATERIALS

1 zippered plastic bag, sandwich size or larger

water

measuring cup

vinegar

1 square of paper towel or a tissue

measuring spoon

baking soda

Why does gas explode? A gas explosion happens when the pressure, or stored energy, builds up within an object or substance. The gas pushes out on the sides of the object until... bang! Try this simple experiment to expand your view on gases.

TIP:
Ask an adult to supervise. This experiment can be messy, so do this in a bathtub, sink, or outdoors.

1   Test the plastic bag by filling it with water. Seal the bag and turn it upside down over a sink or outdoors. Make sure there are no holes or leaks in the bag.

2   Dump the water out of the bag.

3   Using the measuring cup, pour ½ cup (120 milliliters) of vinegar into the plastic bag. Zip the bag shut.

4   Lay the paper towel square or tissue on a flat surface.

5   Use the measuring spoon to measure 4 teaspoons of baking soda. Place the baking soda on the paper towel or tissue.

6   Wrap the sides of the paper towel or tissue around the baking soda to make a small packet.

7 Open the plastic bag and drop the package of baking soda into it. Quickly zip the bag shut.

8 Shake the bag, and set the bag down in the sink or on the ground outdoors. What happens to the bag?

GIVE THIS A TRY:

Come up with ways to try this experiment differently. Consider changing the amount of vinegar or the type of paper to make the packet. Create a table such as the one below to record your data.

Material used:	How long did the fizzing last?	Did the bag pop?
Paper towel		
Tissue		
Tissue paper		

SUPER STRAW

MATERIALS

pear

plastic straw

eraser from
a pencil

orange, lemon,
apple, banana,
potato, or pepper
(optional)

Kitchens are fantastic places to test science experiments. And straws are great for more than just slurping your favorite drink. Is a straw strong enough to pick up a piece of fruit? Get ready to flex your muscles in this test to find out!

1 Hold the pear in one hand and the plastic straw in the other hand.

2 Try to insert the straw into the pear. What happens? You may have made a small dent in the pear, but did the straw go into the fruit easily?

3 Repeat steps 1–2, but this time hold your thumb over the top of the straw. What happens? Were you able to get the straw to stick into the pear and stay by itself?

4 Place the eraser in the tip of the straw.

5 Repeat steps 1–2. Did the straw go into the pear easier or harder?

The end of the straw has a very small surface area. This means the force you apply to the straw is only in a small area. If you tried this with a similar sized object, such as an eraser tip inside the straw, the force would be spread over a larger area. This would be much harder to push into the pear. The key is to push the straw into the fruit quickly. This produces a greater force than if you slowly twist the straw into the fruit.

GIVE THIS A TRY:

Repeat the experiment with an orange, lemon, banana, potato, or a pepper. See how deep you can drive the straw based on the thickness of the food's skin. Consider whether the inside of the fruit or vegetable is solid or filled with air.

SUGAR SUBSTITUTE

MATERIALS

assortment of foods and drinks, including soda, juice, fruits, and vegetables

a list of the amount of sugar in foods

pen and paper

roll of paper towels

sugar cubes, each containing 4 grams of sugar

drinking glass

water

pen and paper

Think about the foods you are eating. Many foods and drinks have sugar added to them. Is the amount of sugar added necessary? Would the food or drink be just as good with less sugar? Your body needs sugar, but too much sugar is not good for you. Let's investigate by comparing different foods and drinks.

TIP:

Have an adult help you look up the amount of sugar in the foods and drinks you selected for your experiment.

1 Gather the foods and drinks you want to test, and lay them on a table in front of you.

2 Split the foods and drinks into three different piles: A. Tastes very sugary, B. Tastes a little sugary, and C. Doesn't taste sugary.

3 Check the sugar content of each food and drink. Write down the sugar content for each of your foods and drinks.

4 In front of each food, place one square of paper towel.

5 Measure out the amount of sugar in each food and drink using the sugar cubes. Place the cubes on the paper towel in front of each food or drink. For example, there are roughly 30 grams of sugar in a can of soda. You would place 8 sugar cubes on the paper towel.

6 Fill the drinking glass $2/3$ full with water.

7 Place the sugar cubes from the soda's pile into the water. Let the cubes dissolve. Take a sip.

8 Now take a sip of the soda. Does the soda taste as sugary as the sugar water?

9 Repeat steps 6–8 for each of the remaining foods and drinks. Write down your observations.

SUGAR, SUGAR

The World Health Organization says that every person should have no more than 5 percent of their daily calories from sugar. That equals about 6 teaspoons (30 grams) per day. Too much added sugar can be bad for you and can cause people to gain weight. Foods that contain natural sugars, such as fruits, vegetables, and whole grain breads, are much better for you.

HOW FAR DOES IT FLY?

Materials

10 craft sticks
4 rubber bands
glue
plastic cap from a soda bottle
marshmallows
meter stick or yardstick
a friend or two

Thanks to the laws of physics, *catapults* hurl heavy objects a long way with great force. Catapults store a lot of energy. The energy is stored in the form of *tension*. You can compare this tension to a bowstring used to shoot a bow. Put your marshmallows to the test, and see how far can you make them fly!

1 Bundle eight craft sticks. Secure each end with a rubber band. You may have to wrap the rubber band around the sticks a few times to get them to stay together.

2 Take the two remaining sticks and make a V around the bundle of eight sticks. One of the sticks will lie flat on the ground, the other stick will be at an angle. Secure one end of the two sticks with a rubber band.

3 Wrap the last rubber band like an X around all of the sticks. You have now created your catapult.

4 Glue the cap from the soda bottle to the craft stick that is sitting up in the air. This is the bucket.

5 Place a marshmallow in the bucket.

6 Push down on the bucket as far as it will go and then release. What happens? The marshmallow probably flies into the air, making an *arc*, and lands on the ground.

catapult—a device used to hurl rocks, liquid, or other items in the air a far distance

tension—the stress on a structure resulting from stretching or pulling

arc—a curved line

7 Hold a competition with your friends. Using the yardstick, see who can fling their marshmallows the farthest!

> The catapult shoots objects at a specific angle. As they fly, they make an arc in the air. You have created a lever, which is used to help lift things or make things fly farther and faster. A lever is a simple machine and is something that is used every day. Examples of a lever are a wheelbarrow, scissors, and even your arm.

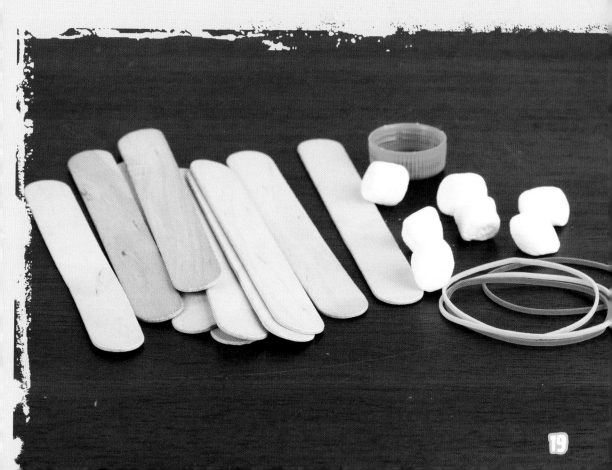

SIMPLY HELPFUL

Simple machines make our lives easier. They help us by transferring a load, changing the direction of a force, and making things easier to lift. They are part of our everyday lives. Examples include screwdrivers, door handles, a wheel and axle in a car, or a ramp that helps people get in and out of buildings.

SINK OR FLOAT?

Materials

scissors

2-liter bottle or other plastic bottle with a small opening

drill

flexible straw

modeling clay

plastic tubing

coins or other small weights

duct tape

a bucket or container 2/3 full of water

Can you name an object that sinks in water but also floats? A submarine, of course! A submarine's ability to both sink and float has to do with *density* and *buoyancy*. See if you can build a boat that seems to defy the laws of buoyancy.

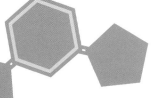

1 With an adult's help, cut 4 small holes on one side of the bottle in a straight line. The holes should be about 1.5 inches (4 cm) apart.

2 With an adult's help, use the drill to make a hole in the bottle cap. Place the straw in the opening in the cap. Wrap the modeling clay around the edge of the opening to secure the straw in place. The straw is your *periscope*.

3 Attach the plastic tubing to the open end of the straw to make the periscope longer.

4 Tape 2 coins or small weights over two of the holes on the bottle.

5 Place your submarine in a container of water with the coins or weights on the bottom of the bottle facing down.

6 Keep the plastic tubing above the water line as your submarine sinks.

The open holes in the bottom of the bottle probably started to bubble. That means that the water is entering the empty bottle and pushing the air that was inside the bottle out. As the water fills up the bottle, the bottle will sink. This is because it is getting heavier and its density is increasing.

density—the amount of mass an object or substance has based on
a unit of volume

buoyant—able to keep afloat

periscope—a device used in a submarine that allows the sailors
inside the vessel to see what is happening above the water

MAKE IT RAIN ACID

Pollution from cars and businesses can build up in the air and cause acid rain and warmer temperatures. You may have heard that acid rain is bad for the environment. What is acid rain anyway? Acid rain is rain that contains *nitric acid* or *sulfuric acid*. The acids get into the rain, snow, or fog from pollution that is in the air. How does acid rain affect plants? Get ready to find out!

MATERIALS

masking tape

marker

4 1-quart jars with lids

4 houseplants

measuring cups

bottle of lemon juice or a bottle of vinegar

water

pen and paper

TIP:

Get an adult's permission to use houseplants because the plants may die. Or go buy inexpensive plants at your local gardening store.

1 Use the masking tape and marker to label each of the jars with one of the following: small amount of acid; medium amount of acid; large amount of acid; water.

2 Repeat step 1 for each of the plants.

3 Place the jars next to the plants of the same name.

4 In the "small amount of acid" jar, pour ¼ cup (60 ml) of lemon juice or vinegar. Fill the rest of the jar with water.

5 In the "medium amount of acid" jar, pour ½ cup (120 ml) of lemon juice or vinegar. Fill the rest of the jar with water.

6 In the "large amount of acid" jar, pour 1 cup (240 ml) of lemon juice or vinegar. Fill the rest of the jar with water.

7 In the "water" jar, fill the jar with water.

8 Place the plants on a windowsill or another location where there is plenty of sunshine.

nitric acid—a colorless, liquid acid that is corrosive

sulfuric acid—a colorless, dense acid that is corrosive

9 Over the next two weeks, water each plant from the jar with the same label every two to four days.

10 Record what happens. Which plant is growing the quickest? The slowest? Are any of the plants dying?

You should see that the plant that is getting only tap water is growing, while the plants that are receiving the acid-water mix are not doing as well. This shows that acid rain can affect the growth of the plants. How do you think acid rain might affect people?

RECYCLING
OLD NEWS

MATERIALS

old picture frame

scissors

wire mesh, like in a window screen

stapler

hammer

sheets of old newspaper

blender or a bowl and spoon

cornstarch

container that is big enough to hold your frame, such as a plastic tub

wooden spoon

aluminum foil

pile of books

We all know that recycling is good for the environment. It is a great way to reduce your ecological footprint. An ecological footprint is how much impact you have on the environment where you live. One way to make your impact smaller is to recycle and reuse instead of throwing something away in the garbage. Get ready to recycle!

GIVE THIS A TRY:

Consider adding color to your paper when it is still wet using food coloring. Or add some glitter or tiny bits of confetti to create a unique sheet of paper.

1 Remove the glass and backing support from the picture frame.

2 Cut a piece of mesh to fit over the frame.

3 Staple the mesh to the back of the frame. If necessary, use the hammer to tap down the staples so that none of them are sticking out.

4 Cut the sheets of newspaper into tiny pieces.

5 If you are using a blender, put the pieces of paper in the blender. Add ½ cup (120 ml) water. Mix the substance until it looks slushy. If you are using a bowl and spoon, let the paper and water sit for a couple of hours, and then stir it up. The mixture should be slushy.

6 Add 2 tablespoons (15 ml) of cornstarch to the paper and water mixture. Stir well.

7 Place your frame into the container or plastic tub.

8 Dump the paper "slush" onto the frame over the mesh.

9 Smooth the slush out with the wooden spoon. Cut a piece of aluminum foil that is as big as the frame. Place the foil on top of the frame.

10 Place the pile of books on the aluminum foil for one hour.

11 Take the books off the foil, and leave the mixture to completely dry overnight. When the mixture dries, you will have a new sheet of paper. Voilà!

ASK QUESTIONS. INVESTIGATE. EXPERIMENT.

These are the things a great scientist does. Science experiments are a great way to explore the world around you. They can teach you about ideas and concepts you might not know. They are also a great way to bust some boredom on a long day. Have some fun experimenting, and you may just be the next Einstein!

GLOSSARY

arc (ARK)—a curved line

buoyant (BOI-uhnt)—able to keep afloat

catapult (KAT-uh-puhlt)—a device used to hurl rocks, liquid, or other items in the air a far distance

data (DAY-tuh)—information or facts

density (DEN-si-tee)—the amount of mass an object or substance has based on a unit of volume

energy (EN-uhr-jee)—the ability to do work, such as moving things or giving heat or light

hypothesis (hye-POTH-uh-siss)—a prediction that can be tested about how a scientific investigation or experiment will turn out

nitric acid (NYE-trik ASS-id)—a colorless, liquid acid that is corrosive

periscope (PER-uh-skope)—a device used in a submarine that allows the sailors inside the vessel to see what is happening above the water

physicist (FIZ-uh-sist)—a person who studies matter and energy

propel (pruh-PEL)—to drive or push something forward

radioactivity (RAY-dee-oh-ak-TIV-uh-tee)—a process in which atoms break apart and create a lot of energy

static electricity (STAH-tik i-lek-TRISS-uh-tee)—the buildup of an electrical charge on the surface of an object

sulfuric acid (suhl-FYOO-ric ASS-id)—a colorless, dense acid that is corrosive

tension (TEN-shuhn)—the stress on a structure resulting from stretching or pulling

READ MORE

Barnham, Kay. *Thomas Edison.* Science Biographies. Chicago: Raintree, 2014.

Thomas, Isabel. *Experiments with Materials.* Read and Experiment. Chicago: Raintree, 2016.

Young, Karen Romano. *Try This!: 50 Fun Experiments for the Mad Scientist in You.* National Geographic Kids. Washington, D.C.: National Geographic, 2014.

INTERNET SITES

FactHound offers a safe, fun way to find Internet sites related to this book. All of the sites on FactHound have been researched by our staff.

Here's all you do:

Visit *www.facthound.com*

Type in this code: 9781515747024

 Check out projects, games and lots more at
www.capstonekids.com

INDEX